ESSENTIAL ELEMENTS

A COMPREHENSIVE BAND METHOD

by

Tom C. Rhodes • Donald Bierschenk • Tim Lautzenheiser • John Higgins

Dear Band Student,

CONGRATULATIONS! You have graduated to the next level of your band experience and are ready to enjoy a new beginning of exciting benefits designed for you and your fellow musicians.

Have you noticed how much better you are playing, counting, listening, and enjoying band? The many hours of quality practice are opening up new opportunities for everyone in your group. You are ready to move to the next level of challenging musical benefits, and they await you in the following pages.

There are so many extra rewards band people enjoy: working together in harmony, performing for parents and friends, having a family of fellow musicians, being recognized by others as a talented person, enjoying a high degree of personal accomplishment, and a treasury of other positive feelings and experiences. You are taking advantage of the chance of a lifetime. Music is the language of the world.

Most importantly, you have chosen to be a part of an organization which has been a proving ground for many of today's most successful people. Your achievements and accomplishments in band are guiding you towards excellence in every part of your life.

We welcome you to Essential Elements Book 2 with the well wishes for continued success on your musical journey. *Strike Up The Band!*

ISBN 0-7935-1268-9

HAL•LEONARD™
CORPORATION
7777 W. BLUEMOUND RD. P.O. BOX 13819 MILWAUKEE, WI 53213

00863519

1. HARMONIZED CONCERT B♭ SCALE   (What is the scale name for your instrument?)

2. THE ASH GROVE

Old Welsh Air

Repeat ▲

3. METER MANIA   Count carefully!

The next line changes to 4/4 ▲

4. SONG OF KITES

Japanese Children's Song

Accidentals   Sharps (♯), flats (♭), or naturals (♮) found in the music but not in the key signature.

5. CHROMATIC CRUISE

►Pay close attention to the accidentals.

6. TECHNIQUE TRAX — Practice slowly at first, then gradually increase your tempo.

7. SALSA SIESTA - Duet — Play all dynamics carefully!

8. RHYTHM ON THE RANGE — Count and clap before playing.

Sightreading — Playing a musical selection for the first time. The key to sightreading success is to know what to look for before playing the piece. Follow the guidelines below, and your band will be sightreading STARS! Use the word **STARS** to remind yourself what to look for before reading a selection the first time.

S — **Sharps or flats** in the **key signature** — Identify the key signature first. Silently practice notes from the key signature. Look for key signature changes in the piece.

T — **Time signature** and **tempo markings** — Identify and look for changes in the piece.

A — **Accidentals** — Check for any accidentals not found in the key signature.

R — **Rhythm** — Slowly count and clap all difficult rhythms. Pay special attention to rests.

S — **Signs** — Look for all signs that indicate dynamics, articulations, tempo changes, repeats, 1st and 2nd endings, and any other instructions printed on your music.

9. SIGHTREADING CHALLENGE #1

4

Balance The proper adjustment of volume and sound from all the instruments in the band playing together. Good balance is achieved when each section of the band can be heard equally. While playing *Balance Builder* listen carefully and follow your director's instructions to make sure your sound blends with the rest of the band.

10. BALANCE BUILDER - Chorale

Adagio ◄ Slow tempo, slower than *Andante*.

History English composer **Thomas Tallis** (1505-1585) served as a royal court composer during the reigns of Henry VIII, Edward VI, Mary and Elizabeth. The great artist, Michaelangelo, painted the Sistine Chapel during Tallis' lifetime. Canons and rounds were among the popular types of 16th century forms of music that Tallis wrote. Divide into groups and play *Tallis Canon* as a four-part round.

11. TALLIS CANON - Round

Thomas Tallis

Andante

Staccato ♩ or ♪ Staccato notes are marked with a dot above or below the note. Play these notes lightly and with separation.

12. STACCATO STEAMBOAT

Moderato

13. PAT - A - PAN

Bernard de la Monnoye

Allegro

Tenuto ♩ or ♪ Tenuto notes are marked with a straight line above or below the note. Play these notes smooth and connected, holding each note for its full value.

14. TENUTO TIME

Andante

Ritardando *(ritard.) (rit.)* Gradually slow the tempo.

15. GLOW WORM

Paul Lincke

Allegretto ◄ A lively tempo, faster than *Andante*, but slower than *Allegro*.

▲Watch your director!

History
Many famous folk songs are about geographical places. The Scottish folk song *Loch Lomond* is one such folk song. Loch (Lake) Lomond is a lake of Scotland renowned for its breathtaking beauty. Located in the southern highlands, it is almost entirely surrounded by hills. One of these is Ben Lomond, a peak 3,192 feet high.

16. LOCH LOMOND

Scottish Folk Song

Moderato

▲ E-natural

rit.

Theory **Key Change** Sometimes a key signature will change in the middle of a piece of music. You will usually see a thin double bar line at a key change. Keep going, making sure you are playing all the correct notes in the new signature.

17. A CHANGE OF KEY

▲Key change

18. CONTRASTS IN B♭ CONCERT

19. ESSENTIAL ELEMENTS QUIZ

Allegretto

rit.

6

34. CONCERT C SCALE EXERCISE (Your C Scale)

35. THE MINSTREL BOY

Irish Folk Song

Theory Syncopation — In many types of music, the accent or emphasis occurs on notes that do not normally receive a strong pulse or beat. This is called **syncopation** and is very common in jazz, rock and pop, as well as in classical music.

36. RHYTHM RAP

37. SYNCOPATION TIME

38. JODIE'S MARCH

History American composer **George M. Cohan** (1878-1942) was also a popular author, producer, director and performer. He helped develop a popular form of American musical theater now known as musical comedy. He is also considered to be one of the most famous composers of American patriotic songs, earning the Congressional Medal of Honor for his works. Many of his songs became morale boosters when the United States entered World War I in 1917.

39. ESSENTIAL ELEMENTS QUIZ - YOU'RE A GRAND OLD FLAG

George M. Cohan

Rallentando *(rall.)* Gradually slow the tempo. (Same as *ritardando*.)

46. WARM - UP CHORALE - Duet

47. IRISH JIG

English composer **Sir Edward Elgar** (1857-1934) received his musical training from his father. Elgar's most famous piece, *Pomp and Circumstance*, was written for the coronation of King Edward VII in 1901, the same year the United States inaugurated its 26th President, Theodore Roosevelt — the youngest man to ever hold the office.

Legato Play in a smooth and connected style, as if all notes were marked with *tenutos*.

48. POMP AND CIRCUMSTANCE - Duet

Sir Edward Elgar

49. TECHNIQUE TRAX

50. ESSENTIAL ELEMENTS QUIZ

12

58. RHYTHM RAP

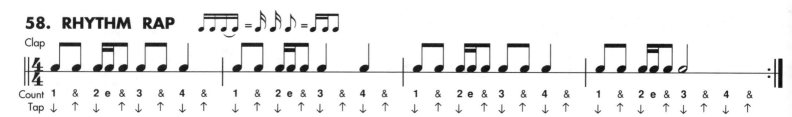

59. RHYTHM ETUDE

Etude A "study piece" designed to teach a specific musical technique.

60. ENGLISH DANCE

Allegretto

61. THE THUNDERER

John Philip Sousa

Allegro

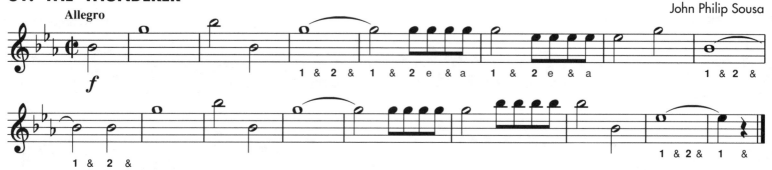

62. CHANGING OF THE GUARD

► Count carefully!

Review the **STARS** guidelines before sightreading.

S — Sharps or flats in the key signature
T — Time signature and tempos
A — Accidentals
R — Rhythm
S — Signs

63. SIGHTREADING CHALLENGE #4

Moderato

French composer **Georges Bizet** (1838-1875) entered the Paris Conservatory to study music when he was only ten years old. There he won many awards for voice, piano, organ, and composition. Bizet is best known for his opera *Carmen*, which was first performed in 1875. *Carmen* showed the new interest of the nineteenth century in the common people; it was about Gypsies and soldiers, smugglers and outlaws. At first people were shocked to see such realism on stage, but *Carmen* was soon hailed as the most popular French opera ever written.

69. TANGO - (LA CUMPARSITA)

Spanish Folk Dance

70. THE YELLOW ROSE OF TEXAS

▲Check the key signature before playing.

71. CONCERT E♭ SCALE AND ARPEGGIO

(Your E♭ Scale)

72. ETUDE IN THIRDS

▲Key change

American composer **John Philip Sousa** (1854-1932) was best known for his brilliant band marches. Although he wrote 136 marches, *The Stars and Stripes Forever* became one of his most famous and was declared the official march of the United States of America in 1987.

73. THE STARS AND STRIPES FOREVER

John Philip Sousa

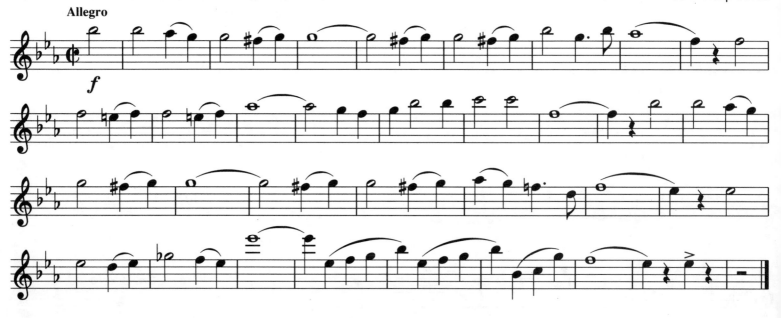

Time Signature
(Meter)

6 - 6 beats per measure
8 - ♪ or 𝄾 gets one beat

♪	= 1 beat
♩	= 2 beats
♩.	= 3 beats
♩.	= 6 beats

There are two ways to count **6/8** time:

6 beats to a measure with the eighth note receiving 1 beat.　　OR　　2 beats to a measure with 3 eighth notes (or its equivalent) receiving one beat.

Slower music is usually counted in 6, while faster music is counted in 2. Start by counting 6 beats to a measure, placing a slight accent on beats 1 and 4 when tapping and counting aloud.

74. RHYTHM RAP

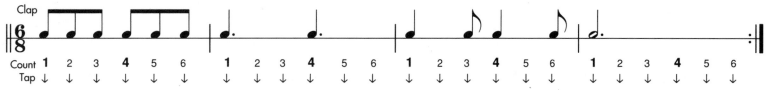

75. LAZY DAY

76. FRENCH FOLK TUNE

Andante

77. ROW YOUR BOAT

The first time through, count and play slowly in 6. Then try playing faster, tapping 2 beats per measure.

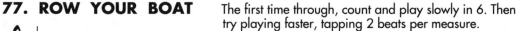

78. JOLLY GOOD FELLOW

▲Pick-up on 6

79. ESSENTIAL ELEMENTS QUIZ - WHEN JOHNNY COMES MARCHING HOME

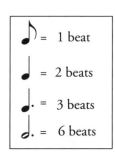

Allegro

mf

1 2 3 4 5 6

▲ Where is beat 6?

16

Theory — Enharmonics

Notes that have different letter names but are fingered the same and sound the same. Here is a reference chart for some common enharmonic notes that you will need to know to play the next few chromatic exercises.

C♯/D♭ C-sharp D-flat D♯/E♭ D-sharp E-flat F♯/G♭ F-sharp G-flat G♯/A♭ G-sharp A-flat

Theory — Chromatic Scale

A scale made up of consecutive half-steps. (A half-step is the smallest distance between 2 notes.) Usually chromatic scales are written with sharps (♯) going up and flats (♭) going down. Practice your chromatic scale to help learn enharmonic notes.

80. CHROMATIC SCALE WARM - UP

Practice slowly at first, until you are sure of all fingerings.

81. TECHNIQUE TRAX

Practice with the following articulation patterns:

A.   B.   C.   D.

History

A **Habañera** is a dance in slow 2/4 meter. It is named after the capital of Cuba, although it was made most popular in Spain during the 1800's by flamenco dancers. One of the most famous Habañeras is heard in Bizet's *Carmen*, written in 1875.

82. HABAÑERA

Georges Bizet

Andante

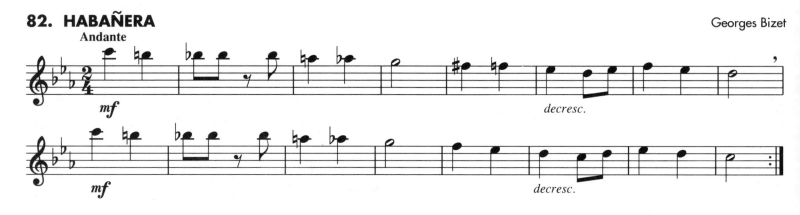

83. CHROMATIC CRESCENDO

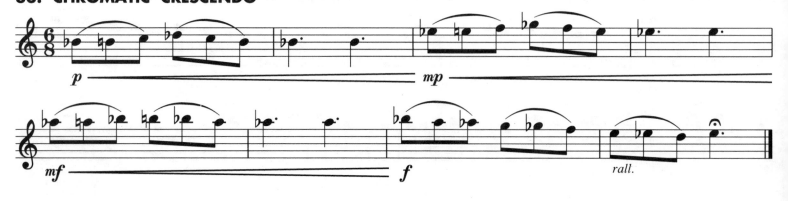

84. TURKISH MARCH
Ludwig van Beethoven

85. THE OVERLANDER
Australian Folk Song

86. STACCATO TIME

Allegro

87. YANKEE DOODLE DANDY
George M. Cohan

Allegro

Review the **STARS** guidelines before sightreading.

S — Sharps or flats in the key signature
T — Time signature and tempos
A — Accidentals
R — Rhythm
S — Signs

88. SIGHTREADING CHALLENGE #5

Andante

Key change!

Triplets A triplet is a group of three notes. In $\frac{2}{4}$, $\frac{3}{4}$, or $\frac{4}{4}$ time, an eighth note triplet is played in one beat.

94. CONCERT F SCALE (Your F Scale)

95. ETUDE IN THIRDS

96. RHYTHM RAP

97. ON THE MOVE

98. CLIMBING HIGHER

99. ARKANSAS TRAVELER Remember to tongue lightly.

100. ESSENTIAL ELEMENTS QUIZ

The Marines' Hymn was written in 1847 during the Mexican War by a Marine Corps poet who set the original lyrics to music from an old French opera. Some of the words refer to the Mexican War. The Treaty of Guadalupe Hidalgo (1848) ended the war. By its terms, Mexico recognized the U.S.'s annexation of Texas and California.

101. THE MARINES' HYMN

102. TECHNIQUE TRAX   Practice slowly at first, then gradually increase the tempo to *Allegro*.

D.S. al Fine   Play until you see the *D.S. al Fine*, then go back to the sign (𝄋) and play until you see the word *Fine* (finish). D.S. is the Latin abbreviation for *Dal segno*, "from the sign."

103. D.S. MARCH

Accelerando *(accel.)*   Gradually increase the tempo.

104. CAN - CAN   Jacques Offenbach

▲Follow your director's accelerating tempo.

114. LISTEN TO THE MOCKINGBIRD   Be sure to tongue lightly.   Alice Hawthorne

Russian composer **Reinhold Gliére** (1875-1956) based his melodies on folk music of the Russian people. Having music reflect the culture of the composer's country was a trend which appeared in much art and music during the late 19th and early 20th centuries. *Russian Sailors' Dance* is an example of such musical Nationalism. It is from his ballet *The Red Poppy*, written in 1927.

115. RUSSIAN SAILORS' DANCE   Reinhold Gliére

▼ Continue playing in the same style.

▼ Go back to the beginning.
D.C. al Fine

116. ANCHORS AWEIGH   Capt. Alfred H. Miles and Charles A. Zimmerman

117. FUNERAL MARCH OF A MARIONETTE   Charles Gounod

► Check all accidentals before playing this piece.

24

Play until you see *D.S. al Coda*, then go back to the sign (𝄋) and play until you see the words "*To Coda.*"
Skip to the *coda* and play until the end. D.S. is the Latin abbreviation for *dal segno*, "from the sign."
Coda means "tail" or conclusion.

118. SIMPLE GIFTS - Full Band Arrangement

Shaker Folk Song
Arr. by John Higgins

119. DANNY BOY - Full Band Arrangement

Arr. by John Higgins

120. SEMPER FIDELIS - Full Band Arrangement

John Philip Sousa
Arr. by John Higgins

121. TAKE ME OUT TO THE BALLGAME - Full Band Arrangement

Arr. by John Higgins

122. SERENGETI (AN AFRICAN RHAPSODY)

By John Higgins

 **Major Scale** A **Major Scale** is a series of eight notes that follow a definite pattern of whole steps and half steps. Half steps appear only between scale steps 3-4 and 7-8. Every major scale has the same arrangement of whole steps and half steps.

123. CONCERT B♭ MAJOR SCALE

124. CONCERT E♭ MAJOR SCALE

125. CONCERT F MAJOR SCALE

126. CONCERT A♭ MAJOR SCALE

127. CONCERT C MAJOR SCALE

128. CONCERT D♭ MAJOR SCALE

129. CONCERT G MAJOR SCALE

130. SPECIAL FLUTE CHROMATIC SCALE

▶ Refer to the fingering chart in the back of the book if you are unsure of any fingerings.

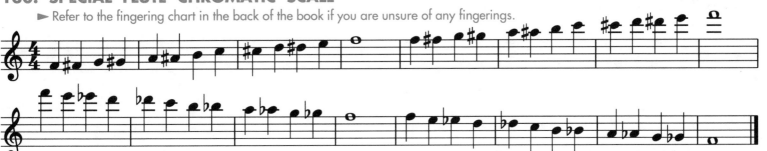

SPECIAL FLUTE EXERCISES

A. TONE DEVELOPMENT EXERCISE

B. OCTAVE STUDY #1

Keep the octave leaps smooth and connected.

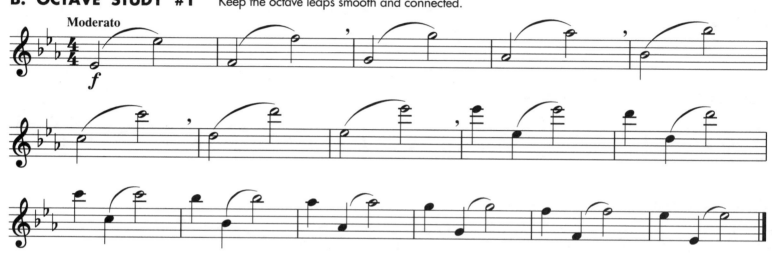

C. OCTAVE STUDY #2

D. ARTICULATION WORK - OUT #1

E. ARTICULATION WORK - OUT #2

F. LEGATO FINGER EXERCISE

G. LOW REGISTER EXCURSION

H. RIGHT HAND EXERCISE

Enharmonic notes. Use the same fingering.

I. INTERVALS

J. ARPEGGIOS

K. ALL NATURAL ETUDE

Check the key signature.

FLUTE FINGERING CHART

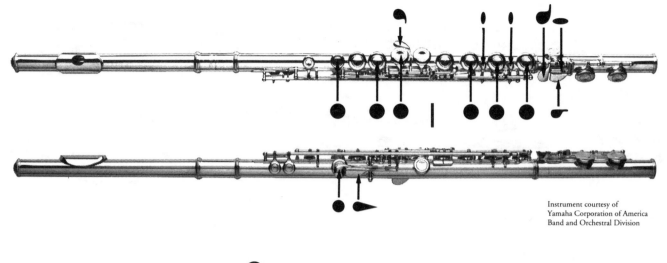

Instrument courtesy of
Yamaha Corporation of America
Band and Orchestral Division

◯ = OPEN

● = PRESSED DOWN

The most common fingering appears on top
when two fingerings are shown.

Take Special Care

Before putting your instrument back in its case after playing, do the following:
- Carefully shake the water out of the head joint.
- Put a clean soft cloth on the end of your cleaning rod.
- Draw the cleaning cloth and rod through the middle and foot joints.
- Carefully wipe the outside of each section to keep the finish clean.

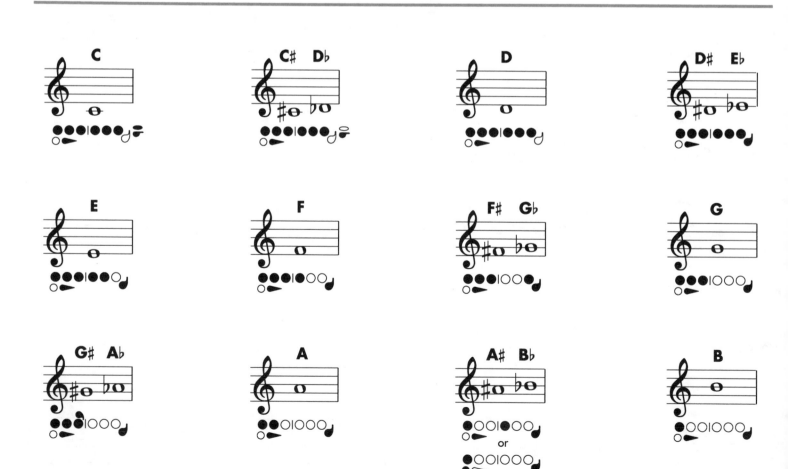

GLOSSARY

Essential Element	Definition
Accelerando *accel.*	Gradually increase the tempo.
Accent	Emphasize the note.
Accidentals	Sharps, flats, and naturals found in the music.
Adagio	Slow tempo, slower than *Andante.*
Alla Breve	Another name for cut time.
Allegretto	A lively tempo.
Allegro	Fast bright tempo.
Andante	Slow walking tempo.
Arpeggio	A sequence of notes from any scale.
Balance	The proper adjustment of volume from all instruments.
Bar Lines	Divide the music staff into measures.
Bass Clef	"F" clef used by trbs., bar, bsn. and tuba.
Bizet, Georges	French composer (1838-1875).
Breath Mark	Take a deep breath after playing the note full value.
Chromatics	Notes that are altered with sharps, flats and naturals.
Chromatic Scale	Sequence of notes in half-steps.
Cohan, George M.	American composer (1878-1942).
Common Time	Another way to write $\frac{4}{4}$.
Crescendo	Gradually increase volume
Cut Time	Meter in which the half note gets one beat.
D.C. al Fine	*Da Capo al Fine* - Play until *D.C. al Fine.* Go back to the beginning and play until *Fine.*
D.S. al Fine	*Del Segno al Fine* - Play until *D.S. al Fine.* Go back to the sign (%) and play until *Fine.*
Decrescendo	Gradually decrease volume.
Dotted Note	The dot adds half the value of the note.
Double Bar	Indicates the end of a piece of music.
Duet	Composition for two players.
Dynamics	The volume of music.
Edgar, Sir Edward	English composer (1857-1934).
Enharmonics	Notes that are written differently but sound the same.
Etude	A "study piece" for a technique.
Fermata	Hold the note longer, or until your director tells you to release it.
1st and 2nd Endings	Play the 1st ending the 1st time through. Then, repeat the same music, skip the 1st ending and play the 2nd.
Flat	Lowers the note and remains in effect the entire measure.
forte *f*	Play loudly.
Gliére, Reinhold	Russian composer (1875-1956).
Habañera	Dance in slow $\frac{2}{4}$ meter.
Half-step	The smallest distance between two notes.
Interval	The numerical distance between two notes.
Key Signature	Flats or sharps next to the clef that apply to entire piece.

Essential Element	Definition
Legato	Play in a smooth and connected style.
Leger Lines	Adds notes outside of the music staff.
Maestoso	Play in a majestic, stately manner.
Major Scale	Series of 8 notes with a definite pattern of whole steps and half steps.
Measure	A segment of music divided by bar lines.
Measure Repeat	Repeat the previous measure.
mezzo forte *mf*	Play moderately loud.
mezzo piano *mp*	Play moderately soft.
Moderato	Moderate tempo.
Multiple Measures Rest	The number indicates how many measures to count and rest.
Music Staff	Lines and spaces where notes are placed.
Natural Sign	Cancels a flat ♭ or sharp ♯ in the measure.
piano *p*	Play softly.
Pick-up Notes	Note or notes that come before the first full measure.
Rallentando *rall.*	Gradually slow the tempo.
Rehearsal Numbers	Measure numbers in squares above the staff.
Repeat Sign	Go back to the beginning and play again.
	Repeat the section of music enclosed by repeat signs.
Rests	Silent beats of music.
Ritardando *rit.*	Gradually slow the tempo.
Round or Canon	Musical form where instruments play the same melody entering at different times.
Sharp ♯	Raises the note and remains in effect the entire measure.
Sightreading	Playing a musical selection for the first time.
Simile *sim.*	Continue in the same style.
Slur	A curved line that connects notes of different pitches.
Sousa, John Philip	American composer (1854-1932).
Staccato	Play the notes with separation.
Strauss, Johann	Austrian composer (1825-1899).
Syncopation	Accents on the weak beats of the music.
Tallis, Thomas	English composer (1505-1585).
Tempo	The speed of music.
Tenuto	Play notes for their full value.
Tie	A curved line that connects notes of the same pitch.
Time Signature (Meter)	Tells how many beats are in each measure and what kind of note gets one beat.
Treble Clef	"G" clef used by fls., ob., clar., sax. and tpt.
Trio	Composition for three players.
Triplet	Group of three notes.
Waltz	Dance in moderate $\frac{3}{4}$ meter.